This story is based on the descriptively enhanced screenplay
developed for "The Animated Stories from the New Testament" video series.
Scripture references have been provided for those readers who
would like to read the story as it is related in the Bible.

Family Entertainment Network, Inc.™
The King Is Born

Matthew 1:18-2:23
Luke 1:26-38; 2:1-40

Stories adapted by:

Sara Clark

Katherine Vawter

Sherry Reeve

Milt Schaffer

Tony Salerno

NEST Publishing
Dallas, texas

It was a sunny day in Jerusalem. A breeze blew through the marketplace where many people shopped. Passing by one of the shops was a woman named Anna. She was on her way to the temple. When she saw an old friend, she called out to him, "Simeon, old man. Why are you here?"

"I'm looking for the Messiah," Simeon said.

"The Redeemer of Israel," she replied.

"The King of the Jews," said Simeon. "I have been promised by the Holy Spirit that I would see Christ the Lord before I die."

Nearby, a spy was hiding in the shadows. When he heard them talk about a new king, he ran to the palace to tell King Herod.

The spy found the evil Herod sitting on his golden throne. He told him what he had heard.

The king became angry and shouted, "These stupid people! They keep looking for a Messiah! I, King Herod, am their Messiah! I am the king of the Jews!"

The spy asked King Herod if he wanted Simeon killed. Herod said, "No! Watch him. If he ever, ever claims to find this Messiah, then the killing will start!"

That same day in Nazareth, a town many miles from Jerusalem, there was a beautiful young woman named Mary. She sang as she worked in her garden.

Suddenly, an angel appeared beside her. "Hail to you, Mary," the angel Gabriel said. "The Lord is with you. And you are blessed among all women."

"Why do you greet me like this, sir?" asked Mary.

"Do not be afraid, Mary," said Gabriel. "For you have found favor with God. You will bring forth a son. His name will be Jesus."

"A son?" Mary asked.

"He will be called the Son of the Highest," Gabriel said. "And the Lord God will give Him the throne of His Father David."

"But how can this be? I am engaged to Joseph the carpenter and we are not married yet," said Mary.

"The holy child you bear is the Son of God. For with God, nothing is impossible," Gabriel said.

Mary knelt in the garden and bowed her head. "I am the Lord's willing servant, sir. Let it happen as you say."

Gabriel left and Mary ran to Joseph's house. Joseph was a strong, handsome carpenter. When he looked up and saw Mary standing at his door, he said, "Mary, come in."

"Joseph, I have something to tell you," said Mary.

"I know everything, Mary. The angel came to me last night. The baby's name will be Jesus," Joseph said.

Mary was so happy. "Oh, Joseph, I was afraid you'd be angry."

"I will be your husband, just as we always planned," said Joseph. "And, I will love this child as if He were my own son."

Mary smiled at Joseph. "I must thank my father for choosing you as my husband."

Later that day, a Roman soldier rode through Nazareth. He was there to deliver a message from Caesar Augustus, the emperor of Rome. "Hear me people of Nazareth," he called out. "A proclamation! Every man must go to the city of his birth! There he will be counted and taxed!"

Everywhere in the Roman empire, soldiers shouted this same command.

Later, after Mary and Joseph were married, they prepared for a journey to obey the emperor's command. They were going to the city of Bethlehem where Joseph had been born.

Joseph knew the trip would be long. He was worried because Mary was going to have the baby soon. He carefully helped her onto a donkey. "Bethlehem is just too far away, Mary," he said.

"But we have no choice," Mary reminded him.

Joseph agreed. "Oh, I know. But it's not safe for you to travel. What if the baby is born along the way?"

Mary smiled. "Then you'll just have to pay the taxes for three instead of two."

Joseph laughed as they started on their way.

For many days and nights Mary and Joseph traveled through the desert and over the mountains. As they neared Bethlehem, Mary said, "Joseph, I think the baby is coming."

"Oh, no!" Joseph said. "We're almost to Bethlehem. Do we have time?"

"A little longer, I think," Mary answered.

When they reached Bethlehem later that evening, Joseph looked for a place to stay. But the small town was full of people who had come to be counted and taxed.

When Joseph stopped at one inn, the innkeeper shouted, "Don't bother me! There's no room here!"

Joseph stammered, "But, sir, my wife is…" The innkeeper slammed the door in his face.

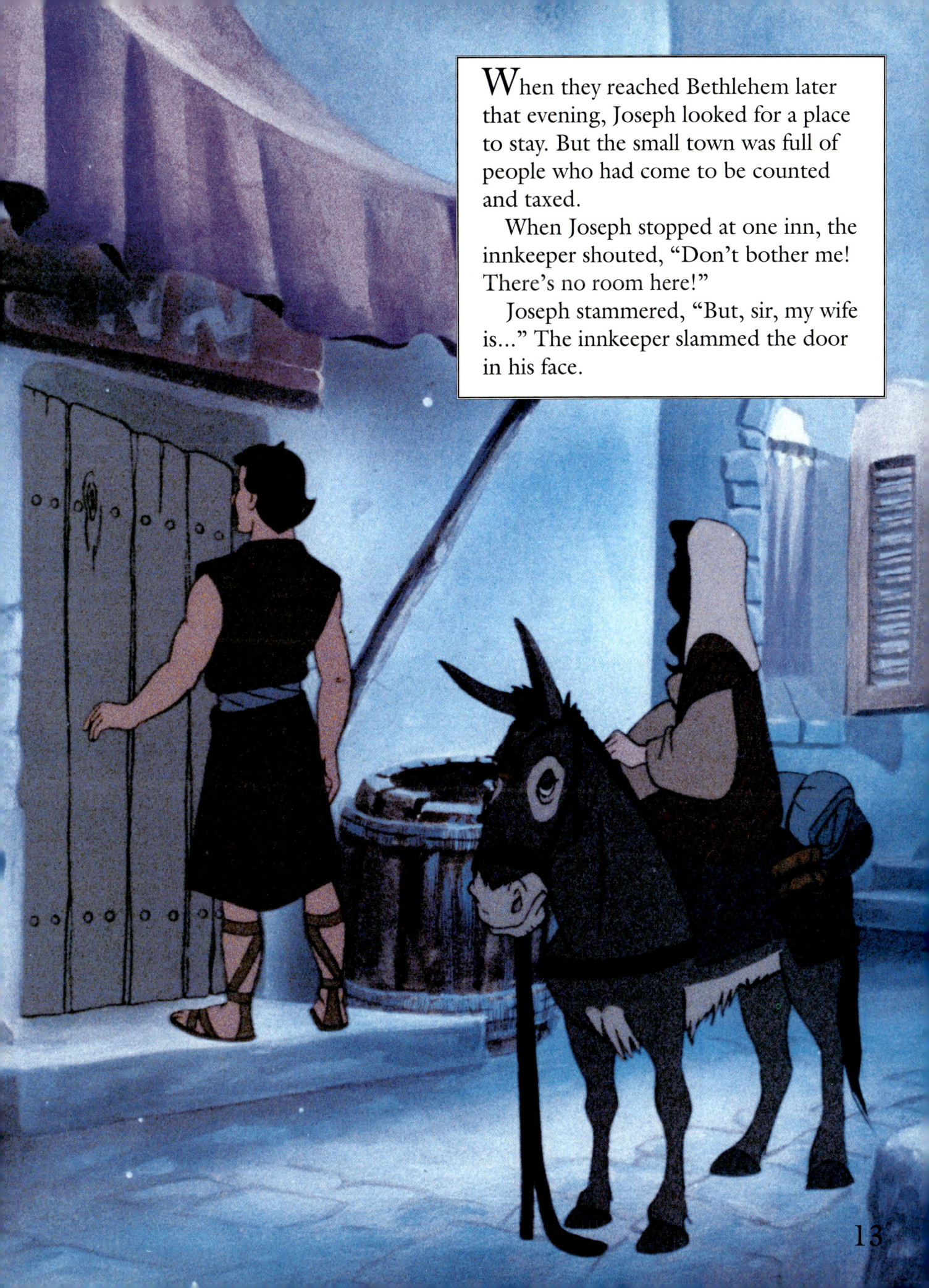

"All the inns seem to be full," said Mary.

"Don't worry, Mary," Joseph said. "We'll find a place."

14

At another inn, Joseph looked inside to see a room crowded with people. He saw a man carrying a tray full of plates and mugs. He called out, "You there! Innkeeper!"

The innkeeper looked at Joseph and said, "I'm sorry, my friend. As you see, I'm full up."

A man shouted, "Hey, innkeeper! Where's my drink?"

The innkeeper found the man's drink on his tray. "Forgive me. My mistake, of course. Thank you for your patience." Then he turned back to Joseph and said, "Not even an inch of floor. I have to walk on my toes to get to the door. Now, goodbye!"

When the innkeeper reached out to shut the door, Joseph stopped it with his hand. "But, sir," he said.

"You're blocking the door," said the innkeeper.

Joseph begged, "Please. Please sir, my wife...The baby is about to..."

"What do you expect me to do? Build a room on the back of the inn tonight?" asked the innkeeper.

Joseph begged again, "But, my wife... the baby..."

"NO ROOM!" shouted the innkeeper, and he slammed the door.

Joseph and Mary had turned to leave when the innkeeper opened the door. "Baby? Baby?" he asked. "Did you say she's about to have a baby?"

Joseph nodded yes.

"Well now, I do have a place for you," the innkeeper said. He motioned for them to follow him. "It's practically a stable. What am I saying? It is a stable. It's a cave, in fact. But it's warm and there's clean straw."

When they got to the stable, Joseph helped Mary down from the donkey onto the soft dirt floor. Joseph said, "We're grateful to you, sir."

The innkeeper walked back to the inn talking to himself. "I just can't say no to anybody, can I? This is no way to run a business. People having babies in the stable. I'm out of my mind," he laughed.

Joseph looked around the dusty, old stable. It was not at all what he had planned. Holding Mary's hand, Joseph whispered, "Mary, don't be afraid."

"I'm not," Mary said softly. "I have you by my side."

Later that night, Jesus was born. The animals in the stable welcomed the special little baby. "Baaa!" "Chirp-chirp!" "Hee-hawww!"

Mary wrapped her newborn son in long bands of cloth called "swaddling." Joseph proudly lifted the baby from her arms. "Jesus. You're here at last. That's all that matters."

Joseph carefully laid the baby in a manger and said, "Sleep now, Mary. He's a strong, beautiful boy."

That evening on a hillside nearby, three shepherds were settling down for the night. Looking toward Bethlehem, the youngest shepherd said, "Look at all those lights in Bethlehem! The city's never been so excited!"

A second shepherd grumbled, "Hush! We're trying to sleep."

"All those people from faraway places!" the shepherd boy said. "Think of all the stories they're telling."

"The stories are all the same," said a third, older shepherd. "The true tales are boring, and the good tales, they're just lies."

The young shepherd boy said, "Well, I still wish I were up there."

"Oh, you better get use to it, young fellow," the older shepherd said. "Nothing important has ever happened in Bethlehem."

The second shepherd rolled over and said, "Now, go to sleep!"

23

Suddenly the dark sky filled with bright light. A choir of angels began to sing, "Glory! Glory!"

Then the angel Gabriel appeared from the heavens and announced, "Fear not! I bring you good tidings of great joy. A message for all people. For unto you is born this day in the city of David, a Savior, which is Christ the Lord. And this will be a sign for you. You will find the baby wrapped in swaddling clothes, lying in a manger."

The angels sang, "Glory to God in the highest. Glory to God in the highest."

Now, the older shepherd was excited. "We must go to Bethlehem at once!"

"But, what about the flock?" the young shepherd boy asked.

"Oh, the sheep will be safe enough," said the older shepherd. "Tonight the Savior of the world is born."

Again the angels sang their praises. "Glory! Glory! Glory to God in the highest. Glory to God in the highest."

Later that evening, the three shepherds found the baby just as Gabriel had said they would. When they saw Jesus, they fell to their knees. They knew they were in the presence of the Son of God.

As the stars twinkled brightly in the sky, the angels sang, "Glory! Glory! Glory to God in the highest. Glory to God in the highest."

That same night, in a land far away, three wise men met in a beautiful palace. One of the men, Caspar, stood on the balcony and looked up into the evening sky. Belthaz and Melchior were inside studying a map of the stars.

"Hmm? Could it be?" asked Belthaz. "Let me see it again."

Melchior pointed to a spot on the map and said, "Well, it is a new star all right. Is this the sign that we have been watching for?"

Belthaz nodded. "It has happened. The birth of the King of heaven."

"You can do what you like, my friends," Caspar said. "But, I want to see this King before I die."

"Let us bring Him gifts," agreed Belthaz.

Melchior opened a chest filled with sparkling coins from his homeland. "The gold of Persia."

Caspar picked up a cloth filled with spice that he had brought from his homeland. "This is sweet-smelling frankincense of Abyssinia."

Belthaz poured a drop of oil into his hand from a jar he had brought from his country. "The myrrh of India, for the newborn King. We have a long journey ahead of us."

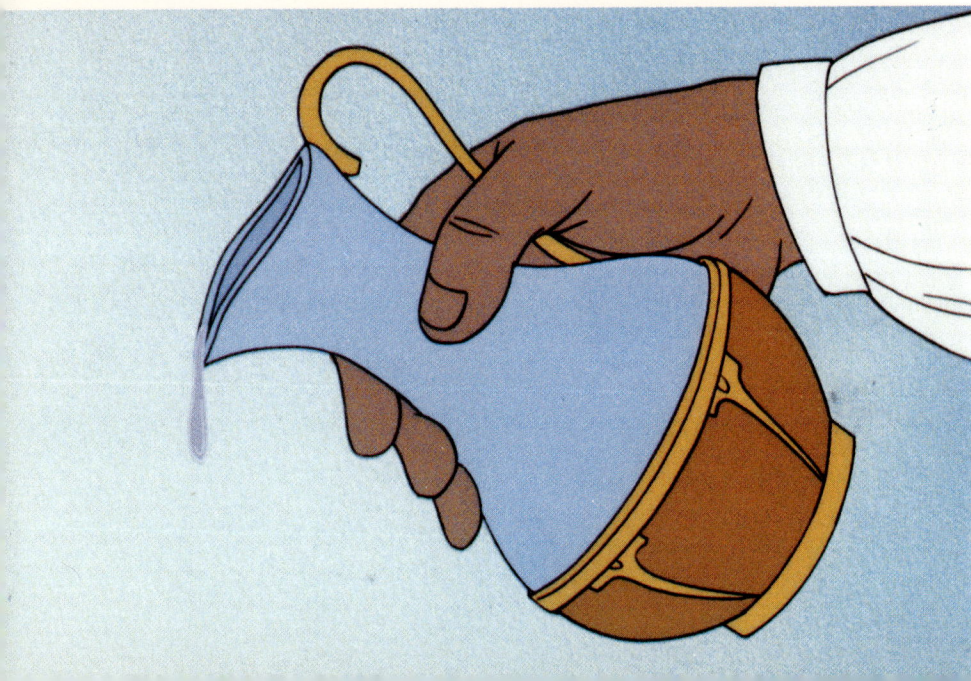

29

The three men gazed up at the bright star in the heavens. Caspar said, "May God speed us on our way."

A few months later Mary and Joseph took Jesus to visit Jerusalem. As they walked through the marketplace, an old man stepped in front of them and cried out, "Stop, sir! Please stop." It was Simeon.

Joseph said, "Sir, please let us by. We've come to present our newborn child to the temple." But Simeon didn't move. "May I look at your sweet baby?"

"His name is Jesus," said Mary kindly.

Simeon looked in amazement at the baby. "I know this child. The Messiah! He is born."

Just then Anna, Simeon's friend, walked up to Joseph and Mary. "Is it Him?" she asked. "Oh, you sweet child, you precious lamb. All of you here at the temple today, give thanks to the Lord! If you look for redemption, here He is. The Redeemer."

"We've come searching among the Jews to find the one who is born to be King," said Caspar.

"We saw His star in the east, the sign of His birth," added Melchior.

"And we have come to worship Him," Belthaz said.

King Herod pretended he was happy. "A newborn king of the Jews?" he asked. "What wonderful news." Then Herod shouted to his servant, "Kadmiel!"

Just then one of Herod's guards announced, "Welcome! The great men of the East."

King Herod dropped the spy and turned to see the three wise men walking toward him. "Ah, yes, yes. What brings you to Palestine?"

Herod thought for a moment. He frowned and stood up from his throne. "But babies grow up, don't they? They grow so quickly. Yes, they do."

The king turned to his spy and asked, "You didn't happen to find out who this baby's parents are? Did you?"

The spy shook his head no.

"Then maybe you found out where this baby lives?" Herod asked.

Once again the spy shook his head.

The king was really angry. He picked the spy up by his collar and shouted, "Fool!"

A short distance away, Herod's spy was again hiding in the shadows. He heard Simeon say, "Lord, now you can let me die in peace. For my eyes have seen salvation." The spy smiled wickedly and ran off to the palace.

The spy told Herod what Simeon had said. The king laughed. "A baby! This Messiah is a baby? What could I possibly fear from a baby?"

The servant ran to Herod's side and bowed. "Why do you summon me, my lord king?"

"Get up," ordered the king. "Didn't you hear what my honored guests are looking for?"

The servant answered, "Yes, the Messiah, right? The one who is born King of the Jews."

"Just where is this Messiah supposed to be born?" King Herod asked.

"Let me see," said Kadmiel, searching through some scrolls. "Ah, here it is. Bethlehem."

"Bethlehem?" Melchior asked.

"Oh, yes. Just a little town south of Jerusalem, called the city of David. Not far. That's the place," answered Kadmiel.

"Thank you," said Melchior. "You have been very helpful."

"Go, my friends," Herod said. "Find this newborn king and bring me word so that I, too, may go and worship Him." But Herod was lying. He only wanted to find out where Jesus was.

"Gladly, King Herod," Belthaz said. "Peace be unto you."

"Peace be unto you, too," Herod said as the three wise men left. Then, Herod angrily said, "A new king? I...I am the king of the Jews!"

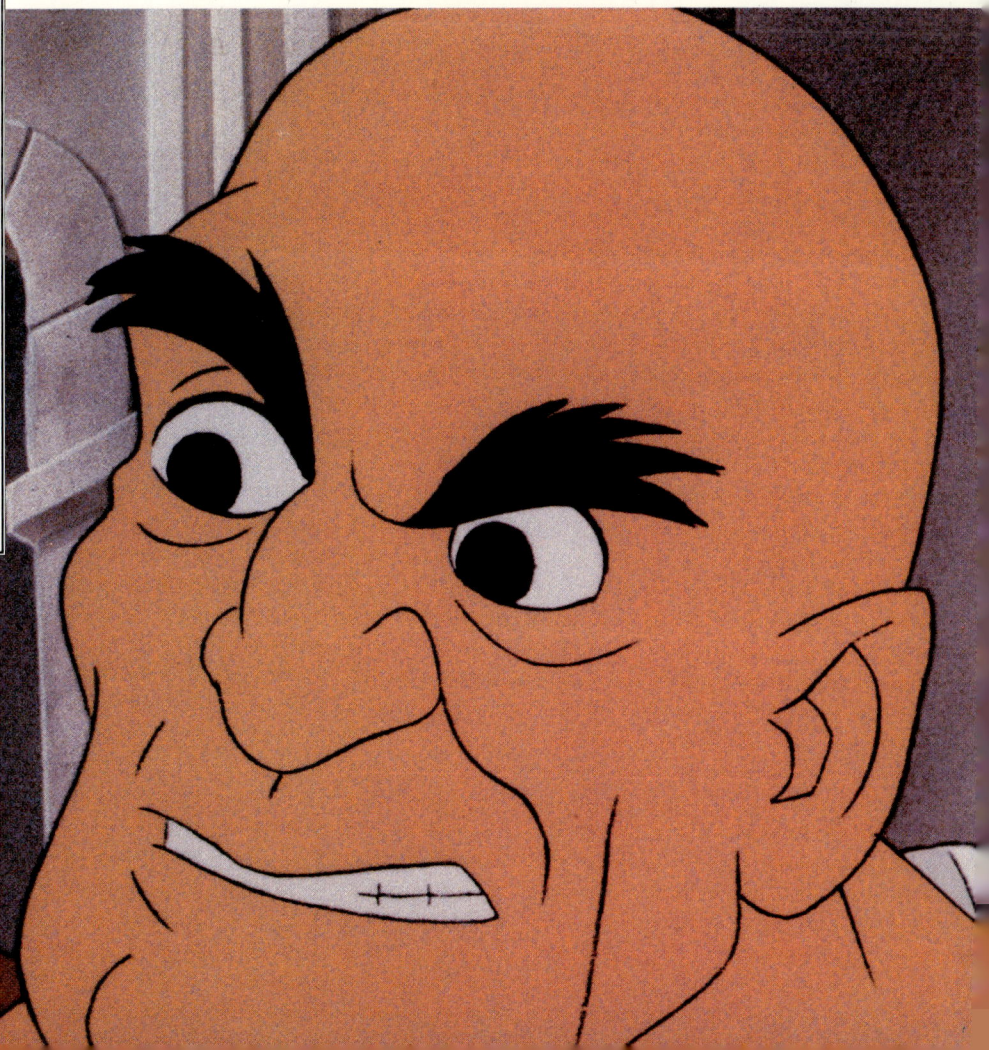

Soon the wise men had traveled from Jerusalem to Bethlehem. There they found the home of Mary and Joseph.

When Mary greeted them, Caspar said, "We have seen the star and followed it here."

"May we see the child of prophecy?" Belthaz asked.

Melchior added, "We have come to honor Him."

"Please, come in," said Mary kindly.

Mary brought the baby to the wise men and Joseph said, "His name is Jesus."

Belthaz looked at the little baby and bowed. "My Lord."

"My King," Melchior added.

"Master," Caspar said.

A few days later at the king's palace, Herod was talking to his spy. "They found Him? Of course they found Him. Why do you think they went home another way? It's all a plot. Against me... ME! But, it won't work, I tell you. It won't work!"

Herod was so angry! "Whoever He is, that boy won't live long enough to challenge me! Do you understand? I am Herod, the ONLY king of the Jews! That child in Bethlehem must die! Kill Him! Kill Him!"

To make sure this would be done, the wicked Herod ordered his soldiers to kill every baby boy two years of age and younger. The soldiers searched each home in Bethlehem hoping to find the baby Jesus.

Parents tried to save their babies, but they could not. The soldiers kicked in doors and knocked the parents down. They did anything to carry out the evil command of the terrible King Herod.

But during that night, while Joseph was sleeping, an angel spoke to him in a dream. "Joseph! Get up! King Herod is searching for the child to destroy Him. You must take the child and His mother to Egypt."

Joseph sat up and said, "Mary! Mary, wake up. We're leaving Bethlehem. Now!"

They dressed quickly and left just before soldiers broke into their house. Mary and Joseph had escaped into the desert. They were on their way to Egypt. They knew that God would protect them.

They stayed in Egypt until the angel of the Lord told Joseph that Herod was dead. Mary and Joseph returned to Nazareth. Jesus grew in spirit, and was filled with wisdom. And the grace of God was upon Him.

THE END

A KING IS BORN

Lyrics by
CAROL LYNN PEARSON

Music by
LEX DE AZEVEDO
Arranged by PAUL FISCHER

With swad-dling for robes and a star for a crown, gen-tly, a King is born. With shep-herds for sub-jects and straw for a throne, to-night a King is born. Born of in-no-cence, born of love; God's love, a gift to all. Bow ev'-ry knee, ev'-ry tongue tell the sto-ry:

Tonight, a King is born.

A mother for love and a mother for birth, gently, a King is born. A Father in heaven, a father on earth, tonight a King is born. Born of innocence, born of love; God's love, a gift to all. Bow ev'ry knee, ev'ry tongue tell the story: Tonight, a King is born.

47

48